EMMANUEL JOSEPH

Above the Desk, Reconstructing Administration in an Evolving World

Copyright © 2025 by Emmanuel Joseph

All rights reserved. No part of this publication may be reproduced, stored or transmitted in any form or by any means, electronic, mechanical, photocopying, recording, scanning, or otherwise without written permission from the publisher. It is illegal to copy this book, post it to a website, or distribute it by any other means without permission.

First edition

This book was professionally typeset on Reedsy. Find out more at reedsy.com

Contents

1. Chapter 1: The Shifting Landscape of Administration — 1
2. Chapter 2: The Human Element in a Digital Age — 3
3. Chapter 3: Redefining Leadership in Administration — 5
4. Chapter 4: The Role of Ethics in Modern Administration — 7
5. Chapter 5: Building Resilient Organizations — 9
6. Chapter 6: The Future of Work and Administration — 11
7. Chapter 7: The Power of Collaboration in Administration — 13
8. Chapter 8: Sustainability and Administration — 15
9. Chapter 9: Innovation in Administration — 17
10. Chapter 10: The Role of Data in Modern Administration — 19
11. Chapter 11: The Global Perspective in Administration — 21
12. Chapter 12: The Path Forward for Administrators — 23

1

Chapter 1: The Shifting Landscape of Administration

The world of administration is no longer confined to the four walls of an office or the rigid structures of traditional hierarchies. As technology advances and global connectivity deepens, the role of administrators has transformed dramatically. Gone are the days when administration was solely about paperwork and compliance. Today, it is about adaptability, foresight, and innovation. Administrators must now navigate a rapidly changing environment where decisions are made in real-time, and the stakes are higher than ever. This chapter explores how the landscape of administration has shifted, emphasizing the need for a new mindset that embraces change rather than resists it.

The rise of digital tools has revolutionized how organizations operate. From cloud-based systems to artificial intelligence, technology has become the backbone of modern administration. However, with these advancements come new challenges. Administrators must now balance the efficiency of automation with the human touch that fosters collaboration and creativity. This chapter delves into the dual role of technology as both a facilitator and a disruptor, urging administrators to harness its potential while remaining vigilant about its limitations.

Globalization has further complicated the administrative landscape. Organizations are no longer bound by geographical borders, and administrators must manage diverse teams across different time zones and cultures. This requires a deep understanding of cultural nuances, communication styles, and global trends. The chapter highlights the importance of cultural intelligence in administration, arguing that success in this new era depends on the ability to bridge gaps and build connections across divides.

The COVID-19 pandemic served as a catalyst for change, forcing organizations to rethink their administrative strategies overnight. Remote work, once a luxury, became a necessity, and administrators had to quickly adapt to this new reality. This chapter examines the lessons learned from the pandemic, emphasizing the importance of resilience and flexibility in administration. It also explores how the crisis accelerated trends that were already underway, such as the shift toward digital transformation and the emphasis on employee well-being.

As the chapter concludes, it sets the stage for the rest of the book by posing a critical question: How can administrators reconstruct their roles to thrive in this evolving world? The answer lies in reimagining administration as a dynamic, forward-thinking discipline that prioritizes innovation, inclusivity, and sustainability. The journey begins with understanding the forces driving change and embracing the opportunities they present.

2

Chapter 2: The Human Element in a Digital Age

In an era dominated by technology, the human element remains the cornerstone of effective administration. While digital tools can streamline processes and enhance productivity, they cannot replace the empathy, intuition, and creativity that humans bring to the table. This chapter explores the delicate balance between technology and humanity, arguing that the most successful administrators are those who leverage technology to amplify human potential rather than replace it.

The rise of automation has sparked fears of job displacement, but this chapter challenges that narrative. Instead of viewing automation as a threat, administrators should see it as an opportunity to focus on higher-value tasks that require critical thinking and emotional intelligence. By delegating repetitive tasks to machines, administrators can dedicate more time to strategic planning, relationship-building, and problem-solving. This shift not only enhances organizational performance but also fosters a more fulfilling work environment.

However, the integration of technology into administration is not without its challenges. One of the most pressing issues is the potential for technology to create a sense of detachment among employees. As interactions become increasingly virtual, administrators must find ways to maintain a sense of connection and community within their teams. This chapter offers practical strategies for fostering engagement in a digital age, from virtual team-building activities to regular check-ins that prioritize open communication.

Another critical aspect of the human element is diversity and inclusion. In a globalized world, administrators must ensure that their organizations reflect the diversity of the communities they serve. This requires a commitment to creating inclusive policies, addressing unconscious biases, and providing opportunities for underrepresented groups. The chapter emphasizes that diversity is not just a moral imperative but also a strategic advantage, as it brings a wider range of perspectives and ideas to the table.

The chapter concludes by underscoring the importance of emotional intelligence in administration. In a world where change is constant, administrators must be able to navigate uncertainty, manage stress, and inspire their teams to persevere. By prioritizing the human element, administrators can create organizations that are not only efficient but also compassionate and resilient.

3

Chapter 3: Redefining Leadership in Administration

Leadership in administration has traditionally been associated with authority and control, but this model is no longer sustainable in an evolving world. Today's administrators must adopt a more collaborative and inclusive approach to leadership, one that empowers others and fosters a culture of shared responsibility. This chapter explores the qualities of effective leadership in modern administration, emphasizing the need for adaptability, empathy, and vision.

One of the key shifts in leadership is the move from a top-down approach to a more decentralized model. In a rapidly changing environment, decisions must be made quickly and at all levels of the organization. This requires administrators to trust their teams and delegate authority, creating a sense of ownership and accountability among employees. The chapter provides examples of organizations that have successfully implemented this model, highlighting the benefits of increased agility and innovation.

Another important aspect of modern leadership is the ability to inspire and motivate others. In a world where uncertainty is the norm, administrators must be able to articulate a clear vision and rally their teams around a common purpose. This chapter explores the role of storytelling in leadership, arguing that compelling narratives can help employees understand the bigger picture and feel connected to the organization's mission.

The chapter also addresses the challenges of leading in a diverse and globalized world. Administrators must be able to navigate cultural differences, manage conflicts, and build bridges across divides. This requires a deep understanding of cultural intelligence and the ability to adapt one's leadership style to different contexts. The chapter offers practical tips for developing these skills, from seeking feedback to engaging in continuous learning.

Finally, the chapter emphasizes the importance of self-awareness in leadership. Administrators must be able to recognize their own strengths and weaknesses, seek out opportunities for growth, and model the behaviors they want to see in others. By leading with humility and authenticity, administrators can build trust and credibility, creating a foundation for long-term success.

4

Chapter 4: The Role of Ethics in Modern Administration

As the world becomes more interconnected, the ethical responsibilities of administrators have grown exponentially. Decisions made in one part of the world can have far-reaching consequences, and administrators must navigate complex moral dilemmas with integrity and transparency. This chapter explores the role of ethics in modern administration, arguing that ethical leadership is not just a moral obligation but also a strategic imperative.

One of the key ethical challenges in administration is balancing competing interests. Administrators must often make decisions that affect a wide range of stakeholders, from employees and customers to shareholders and the broader community. This chapter provides a framework for ethical decision-making, emphasizing the importance of considering the long-term impact of one's actions and prioritizing the greater good.

Another critical issue is the ethical use of technology. As organizations collect and analyze vast amounts of data, administrators must ensure that privacy and security are protected. This chapter explores the ethical implications of data-driven decision-making, from the potential for bias in algorithms to the risks of surveillance and exploitation. It also offers guidelines for using technology responsibly, such as implementing robust data protection policies and promoting transparency.

The chapter also addresses the role of administrators in promoting social and environmental responsibility. In a world facing pressing challenges such as climate change and inequality, organizations have a duty to contribute to the well-being of society. This chapter highlights examples of companies that have integrated sustainability into their operations, demonstrating that ethical administration can drive both social impact and business success.

Finally, the chapter emphasizes the importance of creating a culture of ethics within organizations. Administrators must lead by example, setting the tone for ethical behavior and holding others accountable. This requires ongoing education, open dialogue, and a commitment to continuous improvement. By embedding ethics into the fabric of the organization, administrators can build trust and credibility, ensuring long-term success in an evolving world.

5

Chapter 5: Building Resilient Organizations

In a world characterized by constant change and uncertainty, resilience has become a critical attribute for organizations. Resilient organizations are able to adapt to challenges, recover from setbacks, and emerge stronger than before. This chapter explores the role of administrators in building resilience, emphasizing the importance of proactive planning, flexibility, and a culture of learning.

One of the key components of resilience is the ability to anticipate and prepare for potential disruptions. Administrators must be able to identify risks, develop contingency plans, and ensure that their organizations are equipped to handle crises. This chapter provides practical strategies for risk management, from scenario planning to stress testing, and highlights the importance of staying informed about emerging trends and threats.

Another critical aspect of resilience is the ability to adapt to change. In a rapidly evolving world, organizations must be able to pivot quickly in response to new opportunities and challenges. This requires a culture of innovation and experimentation, where employees are encouraged to take risks and learn from failure. The chapter explores how administrators can foster this culture, from providing resources for innovation to celebrating successes and failures alike.

The chapter also emphasizes the importance of employee well-being in building resilience. Organizations are only as strong as their people, and administrators must prioritize the physical, mental, and emotional health of their teams. This includes creating a supportive work environment, offering resources for stress management, and promoting work-life balance. By investing in their employees, administrators can build a workforce that is not only resilient but also engaged and motivated.

Finally, the chapter highlights the role of leadership in fostering resilience. Administrators must be able to inspire confidence, communicate effectively, and make tough decisions in times of crisis. This requires a combination of emotional intelligence, strategic thinking, and a commitment to the organization's mission. By leading with resilience, administrators can guide their organizations through challenges and position them for long-term success.

6

Chapter 6: The Future of Work and Administration

The future of work is being shaped by technological advancements, demographic shifts, and changing societal expectations. As a result, the role of administrators is evolving in profound ways. This chapter explores the trends that are shaping the future of work and administration, from the rise of remote work to the growing importance of lifelong learning.

One of the most significant trends is the shift toward remote and hybrid work models. The COVID-19 pandemic accelerated this trend, and it is likely to continue in the post-pandemic world. This chapter examines the implications of remote work for administration, from managing virtual teams to maintaining organizational culture. It also offers strategies for overcoming the challenges of remote work, such as fostering collaboration and ensuring accountability.

Another key trend is the increasing demand for skills in areas such as data analysis, digital literacy, and emotional intelligence. As the nature of work changes, administrators must ensure that their teams are equipped with the skills needed to thrive in a digital age. This chapter explores the role of administrators in promoting lifelong learning, from providing training opportunities to creating a culture of continuous improvement.

The chapter also addresses the impact of demographic shifts on the future of work. As the workforce becomes more diverse in terms of age, gender, and background, administrators must be able to manage multigenerational teams and create inclusive work environments. This requires a deep understanding of the needs and expectations of different groups, as well as a commitment to fostering diversity and inclusion.

Finally, the chapter explores the role of administrators in shaping the future of work. By embracing innovation, promoting sustainability, and prioritizing employee well-being, administrators can create organizations that are not only successful but also socially responsible. The chapter concludes by urging administrators to take a proactive approach to the future, using their skills and influence to drive positive change in the world of work.

7

Chapter 7: The Power of Collaboration in Administration

Collaboration has always been a cornerstone of effective administration, but in an evolving world, its importance has grown exponentially. As organizations become more complex and interconnected, administrators must be able to work across boundaries, both within and outside their organizations. This chapter explores the power of collaboration in administration, emphasizing the need for partnerships, teamwork, and shared goals.

One of the key benefits of collaboration is the ability to leverage diverse perspectives and expertise. By bringing together individuals with different backgrounds, skills, and experiences, administrators can generate innovative solutions to complex problems. This chapter provides examples of successful collaborations, from cross-functional teams to public-private partnerships, and highlights the role of administrators in fostering a collaborative culture.

Another important aspect of collaboration is the ability to build trust and rapport with others. In a world where relationships are increasingly virtual, administrators must find ways to establish and maintain connections with colleagues, partners, and stakeholders. This chapter offers practical strategies for building trust, from active listening to transparent communication.

The chapter also addresses the challenges of collaboration, such as managing conflicts and aligning priorities. Administrators must be able to navigate these challenges with diplomacy and tact, ensuring that all parties feel heard and valued. This requires strong interpersonal skills, as well as a commitment to finding common ground.

Finally, the chapter emphasizes the role of collaboration in driving organizational success. By working together, administrators can achieve more than they could on their own, creating value for their organizations and the broader community. The chapter concludes by urging administrators to embrace collaboration as a core principle of their work, recognizing that in an evolving world, no one can succeed alone.

8

Chapter 8: Sustainability and Administration

Sustainability has become a critical concern for organizations around the world, and administrators play a key role in driving sustainable practices. From reducing carbon footprints to promoting social responsibility, administrators must integrate sustainability into every aspect of their work. This chapter explores the intersection of sustainability and administration, emphasizing the need for long-term thinking and holistic approaches.

One of the key challenges in sustainability is balancing economic, environmental, and social goals. Administrators must be able to make decisions that benefit all three dimensions, ensuring that their organizations thrive without compromising the well-being of future generations. This chapter provides a framework for sustainable decision-making, emphasizing the importance of considering the full lifecycle of products and services.

Another important aspect of sustainability is the role of technology in driving positive change. From renewable energy to smart cities, technology has the potential to transform the way organizations operate and interact with the environment. This chapter explores the opportunities and challenges of using technology for sustainability, from reducing waste to improving efficiency.

The chapter also addresses the role of administrators in promoting sustainability within their organizations. This includes setting sustainability goals, measuring progress, and engaging employees in sustainability initiatives. By creating a culture of sustainability, administrators can ensure that their organizations are not only environmentally responsible but also socially and economically resilient.

Finally, the chapter emphasizes the importance of collaboration in achieving sustainability goals. Administrators must work with a wide range of stakeholders, from government agencies to community groups, to drive systemic change. The chapter concludes by urging administrators to take a leadership role in sustainability, recognizing that their actions today will shape the world of tomorrow.

9

Chapter 9: Innovation in Administration

Innovation is the lifeblood of progress, and in an evolving world, it is essential for administrators to embrace a culture of innovation. From streamlining processes to developing new products and services, innovation can drive organizational success and create value for stakeholders. This chapter explores the role of innovation in administration, emphasizing the need for creativity, experimentation, and a willingness to take risks.

One of the key drivers of innovation is the ability to think outside the box. Administrators must be able to challenge conventional wisdom, explore new ideas, and embrace change. This chapter provides examples of innovative practices in administration, from agile methodologies to design thinking, and highlights the role of administrators in fostering a culture of innovation.

Another important aspect of innovation is the ability to learn from failure. In a world where change is constant, not every idea will succeed, and administrators must be able to view failure as an opportunity for growth. This chapter explores the importance of creating a safe environment for experimentation, where employees feel empowered to take risks and learn from their mistakes.

The chapter also addresses the role of technology in driving innovation. From artificial intelligence to blockchain, technology has the potential to transform the way organizations operate and deliver value. This chapter explores the opportunities and challenges of using technology for innovation, from enhancing productivity to creating new business models.

Finally, the chapter emphasizes the importance of collaboration in fostering innovation. By bringing together diverse perspectives and expertise, administrators can generate new ideas and solutions that drive organizational success. The chapter concludes by urging administrators to embrace innovation as a core principle of their work, recognizing that in an evolving world, innovation is the key to staying ahead.

10

Chapter 10: The Role of Data in Modern Administration

Data has become one of the most valuable resources in modern administration, providing insights that drive decision-making and improve organizational performance. However, with great power comes great responsibility, and administrators must be able to use data ethically and effectively. This chapter explores the role of data in modern administration, emphasizing the need for data literacy, transparency, and accountability.

One of the key benefits of data is its ability to provide a factual basis for decision-making. By analyzing data, administrators can identify trends, uncover opportunities, and mitigate risks. This chapter provides examples of data-driven decision-making in administration, from performance metrics to predictive analytics, and highlights the importance of using data to inform strategy.

Another important aspect of data is its role in enhancing transparency and accountability. By making data accessible to stakeholders, administrators can build trust and credibility, ensuring that their organizations are held to high standards. This chapter explores the challenges of data transparency, from ensuring data accuracy to protecting privacy, and offers strategies for overcoming these challenges.

The chapter also addresses the ethical implications of data use in administration. From bias in algorithms to the risks of surveillance, administrators must be vigilant about the potential for data to be misused. This chapter provides guidelines for using data ethically, from implementing robust data protection policies to promoting transparency and accountability.

Finally, the chapter emphasizes the importance of data literacy in modern administration. Administrators must be able to understand and interpret data, as well as communicate its implications to others. The chapter concludes by urging administrators to invest in data literacy, recognizing that in an evolving world, data is a critical tool for success.

11

Chapter 11: The Global Perspective in Administration

In an increasingly interconnected world, administrators must adopt a global perspective in their work. From managing international teams to navigating global markets, the ability to think and act globally is essential for success. This chapter explores the role of a global perspective in administration, emphasizing the need for cultural intelligence, adaptability, and a commitment to global citizenship.

One of the key challenges of global administration is managing diversity. Administrators must be able to navigate cultural differences, communicate effectively across borders, and build inclusive teams. This chapter provides practical strategies for managing diversity, from cultural training to cross-cultural communication, and highlights the importance of fostering a global mindset.

Another important aspect of global administration is the ability to adapt to different regulatory environments. From tax laws to labor standards, administrators must be able to navigate the complexities of operating in multiple jurisdictions. This chapter explores the challenges of global compliance, from understanding local regulations to managing cross-border transactions, and offers strategies for overcoming these challenges.

The chapter also addresses the role of administrators in promoting global citizenship. In a world facing pressing challenges such as climate change and inequality, organizations have a responsibility to contribute to the well-being of the global community. This chapter highlights examples of companies that have embraced global citizenship, demonstrating that ethical administration can drive both social impact and business success.

Finally, the chapter emphasizes the importance of collaboration in global administration. By working with international partners, administrators can achieve more than they could on their own, creating value for their organizations and the broader community. The chapter concludes by urging administrators to embrace a global perspective, recognizing that in an evolving world, success depends on the ability to think and act globally.

12

Chapter 12: The Path Forward for Administrators

As the world continues to evolve, the role of administrators will become increasingly complex and demanding. To thrive in this new era, administrators must be willing to embrace change, challenge the status quo, and lead with vision and integrity. This final chapter explores the path forward for administrators, emphasizing the need for continuous learning, adaptability, and a commitment to making a positive impact.

One of the key themes of this chapter is the importance of lifelong learning. In a world where change is constant, administrators must be able to acquire new skills, stay informed about emerging trends, and adapt to new challenges. This chapter provides practical strategies for continuous learning, from seeking out mentors to engaging in professional development opportunities.

Another important theme is the need for administrators to lead with purpose. In a world facing pressing challenges such as climate change and inequality, administrators have a responsibility to use their skills and influence to drive positive change. This chapter explores the role of administrators as change agents, from promoting sustainability to fostering diversity and inclusion.

The chapter also emphasizes the importance of resilience in the face of uncertainty. Administrators must be able to navigate challenges, recover from setbacks, and emerge stronger than before. This requires a combination of emotional intelligence, strategic thinking, and a commitment to the organization's mission.

Finally, the chapter concludes by urging administrators to embrace the opportunities of an evolving world. By reimagining their roles, prioritizing innovation, and leading with integrity, administrators can create organizations that are not only successful but also socially responsible. The journey ahead is challenging, but with the right mindset and skills, administrators can shape a brighter future for themselves, their organizations, and the world.

Book Description: Beyond the Desk: Reconstructing Administration in an Evolving World

In a world that is changing faster than ever, the role of administration is no longer confined to paperwork, rigid structures, or traditional hierarchies. *Beyond the Desk: Reconstructing Administration in an Evolving World* is a thought-provoking exploration of how administrators can adapt, innovate, and lead in an era defined by technological disruption, globalization, and shifting societal expectations.

This book takes readers on a journey through the challenges and opportunities facing modern administrators. From the rise of remote work and the ethical use of technology to the importance of sustainability and cultural intelligence, each chapter delves into a critical aspect of administration in the 21st century. Through practical insights, real-world examples, and actionable strategies, the book provides a roadmap for administrators to thrive in an increasingly complex and interconnected world.

At its core, *Beyond the Desk* is a call to action for administrators to rethink their roles and embrace a more dynamic, forward-thinking approach. It emphasizes the importance of balancing efficiency with empathy, leveraging technology while preserving the human element, and leading with integrity in the face of uncertainty. Whether you are a seasoned administrator or new to the field, this book offers valuable lessons on how to navigate change, foster collaboration, and drive meaningful impact.

Written in an engaging and accessible style, *Beyond the Desk* is not just a guide—it's an invitation to reimagine what administration can be. It

CHAPTER 12: THE PATH FORWARD FOR ADMINISTRATORS

challenges readers to move beyond the confines of traditional practices and embrace a future where adaptability, innovation, and purpose are at the heart of their work.

For anyone looking to stay ahead in a rapidly evolving world, *Beyond the Desk: Reconstructing Administration in an Evolving World* is an essential read. It's a testament to the power of administration as a force for positive change and a reminder that, even in the face of uncertainty, the future is full of possibilities.